The

NUTCRACKER

A Story & A Ballet

THE NUT

A Story & A Ballet

Photographs by

Atheneum

CRACKER

by Ellen Switzer

Steven Caras & Costas

New York 1985

Library of Congress Cataloging in Publication Data

Switzer, Ellen.
The Nutcracker.

SUMMARY: Describes the Tchaikovsky ballet,
the Hoffmann story on which it was based,
and the version staged by the New York City Ballet,
as shown through photographs
and interviews with some of the dancers.
1. The nutcracker (Ballet)—Juvenile literature.
2. New York City Ballet—Juvenile literature. [1. The
nutcracker (Ballet) 2. New York City Ballet.
3. Ballet] I. Costas, ill. II. Caras, Steven, ill.
III. Title.
GV1790.N8S92 1985 792.8'42 85-7463
ISBN 0-689-31061-7

Published simultaneously in Canada by Collier Macmillan Canada, Inc.
Text set by Linoprint Composition, New York City
Printed and bound by South China Printing Company, Hong Kong
Designed by Mary Ahern
First American Edition

CONTENTS

The
NUTCRACKER
A Story & A Ballet

THE
NUTCRACKER

As a Story

When I was nine years old, I met my first Nutcracker. He was in an illustrated book that I had taken from my father's library. Like the Stahlbaums, in whose home the Nutcracker story takes place, we were living in Germany in a big house with many dark corners and huge old trees all around. On nights when the moon was bright and the wind was blowing, the branches of those trees made moving shadows on my white bedroom walls. Often they looked like oversized bats, or owls, or other night creatures, who had invaded the house and were flapping their wings at me.

On such nights I would often sneak downstairs to pick out a book to take to bed and read under the covers, with the help of a flashlight, hoping that nobody would discover that I wasn't sleeping. Reading after lights-out was not encouraged in my family.

I picked out E.T.A. Hoffmann's *The Nutcracker and the Mouse King* because of the picture of the hero on the book jacket. The Nutcracker looked like such a friendly little fellow with his long red nose, his shiny white teeth, his prominent green eyes, and his white hair and beard, all dressed up in a smart-looking soldier's uniform. The book seemed like the perfect choice to banish the fears of a cold, lonely, and windy night. It wasn't. Although the story fascinated me, so that I did not stop reading until long after midnight, it also frightened me into a month of nightmares.

I really couldn't quite make out why that book was so terrifying. On the surface it was just one more fairy tale, like so many I had read over the years. But somehow I knew that this story was different from "Sleeping Beauty" or "Snow White" or "The Princess and the Frog Prince." It had mysterious hidden meanings I could not understand and wasn't at all sure I wanted to.

Many years later, when I started to work on this book, I learned that the author had not meant this particular fairy tale, which was published in 1816, to be a story for children. As a matter of fact, in a brief discussion with friends, the character who tells the story (and who is clearly a stand-in for Hoffmann) says specifically that no one should mistake this particular tale as a bedtime story for a child. It would be, he assured his listeners, much too frightening.

The ballet story, although based on the Hoffmann tale, is very different, as we will see in the next chapter. It, indeed, is meant for children as well as adults and is full of love and warmth and laughter and delight. But the original had none of these qualities. Full of dark undertones, it is a story told by a man who had a very bleak opinion of human nature in general, and family relationships in particular.

I also began to understand, as I reread it, that the mysterious, dark quality of the story, its irony and its double and triple meanings, showed an amazing literary craftsmanship, an ability to create atmosphere and emotion unusual in German stories of Hoffmann's time. Eventually he was recognized as a highly original writer and became a model for many European and American writers who specialized in mystery and horror. Edgar Allen Poe, the nineteenth century American master of horror stories that managed to frighten more people than any slasher TV show or movie of today, admired Hoffmann and said that he had learned a great deal from him. However, Hoffmann was right. He was not a children's book writer.

Basically the Hoffmann *Nutcracker* is a story within a story. The main plot is about a little girl called Marie, who is near the age I was at the time I read the book. She lived with a family, superficially just like mine (she even had a brother), in a house much like mine in Germany. But everything about that family was different from mine. No one in Marie's family seemed to love anyone, except for the strange love that Marie felt for her nutcracker doll. No one seemed to trust anyone. Marie is pictured as an innocent among a group of cynical adults.

At the beginning of the story, Marie is a child. At a Christmas party, Marie receives the Nutcracker from Drosselmeier. Incidentally, Drosselmeier does not appear with his nephew as he does in the ballet. He comes alone. In this first scene, he seems kind and genuinely fond of Marie, but one gets the impression that he is also slightly contemptuous of her and of everyone else in the family.

At night, when the party is over, hundreds of mice appear from cracks and crannies in the room, lead by the vicious Mouse King with seven heads, who blackmails Marie into giving him all her prized marzipan dolls by threatening to dismember the Nutcracker. Eventually the Nutcracker attempts to fight him, but is almost immediately overcome. Marie throws her slipper at the Mouse King and promptly faints dead away. There is no definite outcome to the battle. The next time we see Marie, she is lying in a pool of blood, surrounded by her family and attended by a physician. It seems that a toy cabinet with glass doors has fallen on her and has severely cut her arm, so that she almost bled to death.

The family is thoroughly unsympathetic. "What was she doing downstairs at the cabinet in the first place?" they want to know. She is a disobedient child, who should have been in bed. Getting seriously injured was no more than she deserved. When she tells them the story of the mice and the Nutcracker, they accuse her of lying and threaten to destroy all her toys (including the Nutcracker), unless she admits that she is a bad, untruthful child.

Herr Drosselmeier comes to see Marie while she is still weak and sick and tells her and her brother a story about the beginning of the feud between the Mouse King's family and the Nutcracker. That story seems like a traditional fairy tale turned inside out. In many of the tales we all know, a king and queen have a beautiful young daughter who is cursed by an evil witch, to be rescued later by a handsome and brave prince. They fall in love and live happily ever after.

But that is not the way it happens in the Hoffmann story. There is indeed a beautiful baby princess called Pirlipat, who is cursed to become repellently ugly by the Mouse King's mother. She is avenging the death of several of her sons at the hands of the King, Pirlipat's father. The only way for the princess to be freed from the curse of extreme ugliness is for someone to find the hardest nut in the world and for a brave and handsome young man to crack it with his teeth and to give the kernel to the princess to eat.

The King commissions his court clockmaker and resident wise man, who is also called Drosselmeier (presumably he is an ancestor of Marie's godfather), to find the nut with the help of the court astrologer. If they don't find it, they will be beheaded.

The two men search the whole world with no success and finally return to their home city of Nuremberg, resigned to death. But miracle of miracles, the one existing specimen of the nut is actually in that city. It is owned by Drosselmeier's nephew, a very handsome young man whom any princess might love. The king, meanwhile, has promised that any young man who lifts the curse of ugliness from his daughter by cracking the nut will be given her hand in marriage.

So young Drosselmeier goes to the palace, sees the horrid-looking princess, and feels nothing but love and pity for her, even though most people turn away their eyes when she enters a room. He cracks the nut and gives her the kernel. The second she has swallowed it, she turns into the most beautiful young woman in the world. But young Drosselmeier has now inherited the curse, although nobody bothered to tell anyone that this would inevitably happen. He becomes repulsively ugly; indeed, he looks like a wooden nutcracker instead of a beautiful young man. And this is where the Hoffmann story begins to differ from any of the classical fairy tales we all know. The princess does not kiss him gratefully and tell him that, because he is so brave and kind, his altered looks don't matter. She shrieks in horror and asks her father to have the royal bouncer throw the unattractive young man out the door and down the castle steps. If he ever comes back, he is told, he will be executed.

The clockmaker and the astrologer, who had been promised riches beyond their wildest dreams if they did their part to save the princess, are also forcibly removed from the castle without any reward. The king curses them and tells them that if they don't leave the country, he will have them killed, too.

In all the commotion, young Drosselmeier accidentally steps

on the Mouse King's mother, who had come out of her hole in the floor to watch the proceedings, and kills her. The Mouse King swears eternal vengeance on the Nutcracker. That's the end of Drosselmeier's story.

There is, of course, as much obvious violence and villany in traditional fairy tales as in the Hoffmann story, but in the end, the good, the kind, and the loving always win. With Hoffmann's story, characters with these qualities lose. The wise clockmaker and astrologer were banished forever from the home they loved. And the Nutcracker, rejected not only by the princess, but by all his former friends, wandered off to a lonely and loveless life.

The tale is told in a very straightforward manner, but Hoffmann's bitterness, his contempt for human nature in general, and for authority figures in particular, is evident in every line. Though there is the suggestion that the Nutcracker might turn out to be a handsome prince someday, if a beautiful young girl will love him in spite of his ugliness, this doesn't seem very likely.

Hoffmann then switches back to the main story, having explained through the subplot why the Mouse King is the Nutcracker's enemy. There is another battle, and this time, without Marie's help, the Nutcracker kills the Mouse King. Then the Nutcracker and Marie go off on a wonderful journey through the Land of the Dolls, the Christmas Wood, finally coming to the capitol of the kingdom called Candytown. It turns out that the Nutcracker is a prince in that country, and he is welcomed by loyal subjects and grateful relatives.

At the end of a lovely evening, Marie is wafted into the air and plopped down in her own little bed in Nuremberg. Her mother wakes her up by warning her angrily that she has missed breakfast. When Marie tries to tell the story of her new adventure, she is again ridiculed, scolded, and threatened with punishment if she does not stop telling lies. Her brother calls her "a silly goose," and Herr Drosselmeier makes a stern face, mutters "stuff and nonsense," and accuses her of taking his watch chain ornament—a little gold crown the Nutcracker gave her as a reward for her loyalty. Marie knows that she is only safe if she keeps her memories and feelings to herself. Although in the center of a family, she is all alone...just like the Nutcracker after the Princess rejected him.

In the last two paragraphs of the story, she meets and marries Herr Drosselmeier's nephew, and he takes her off to his country where he may or may not be a prince. The ending does not fit with the rest of the story either by logic (Marie is much too young to be getting married within a few weeks of that Christmas party), or in philosophy and motivation. It seemed unbelievable when I was nine years old, and it seems just as unbelievable now.

When one reads about E.T.A. Hoffmann's life, the reasons for his bitterness become clear. He was a man who loved beauty, but who was physically so unattractive that many of his contemporaries remarked on his ugly appearance. He was small and wizened (like the Nutcracker) and had a large nose and a very long chin that jutted out at almost right angles from his face. He was an artist as well as a writer, and in a German museum there is one self-portrait that he drew at about the time he wrote the Nutcracker story. It makes him look almost spectacularly ugly and shows his self-contempt.

Interestingly enough, several of the dancers who have taken the role of Drosselmeier over the years (including George Balanchine) have used makeup that made them look a great deal like that self-portrait of Hoffmann, softened considerably to make their faces look kinder and gentler than that in the drawing.

Even Hoffmann's dim view of family relationships is

9

reflected in his own life. His parents were divorced when he was about seven years old, an occurance that must have caused a huge scandal in that very conservative time and place. He never saw much of his father after the separation, and his mother let him know repeatedly, and in no uncertain terms, that she considered him a disappointment. She spent as little time with him as possible, and he was left to his own devices at a very early age. Eventually he married, but his marriage was apparently not much happier than his parent's, although he did not divorce his wife.

So, like Marie, he must have often felt isolated in a world that did not understand him, considered him an outsider, and rejected him, like the Nutcracker, because he was not handsome or glamorous.

Many years after Hoffmann's death, when his story had generally been forgotten, Alexander Dumas (the father...he had a son who was also a famous writer), adapted the tale specifically as a children's story, eliminating much of the bitterness and confusion. However, without these qualities, the complex structure with the two interlocking tales did not really make sense.

The Dumas *Nutcracker* was apparently read with interest by Marius Petipas, senior ballet master of the Russian Imperial Ballet, who commissioned Peter Ilyich Tchaikovsky to compose a score for a full length *Nutcracker* production. By the time the music was completed, Petipas was too sick to choreograph the work. It was turned over to Lev Ivanov, who followed Petipas as the most important ballet master at the Russian court.

Both the composer and the two ballet masters realized that the Nutcracker story had to be simplified to be suitable for a ballet, so the entire subplot about Princess Pirlipat and the hard nut was dropped. It was from this version that George Balanchine created his Nutcracker ballet.

THE
NUTCRACKER

As a Ballet

*O*n Tuesday evening, December 8, 1983, the curtain at the New York State Theater rose for the one thousandth performance of the *Nutcracker,* as choreographed by George Balanchine and danced by the New York City Ballet. Almost everyone who knows the Company expects that sometime around the turn of this century there will be a two thousandth performance. *The Nutcracker* is not only an all-time ballet masterpiece, it is also a unique spectacle, a Christmas tradition, and an enduring hit.

In every audience during *The Nutcracker* season there are adults (who have sent for their tickets months before the actual performance) bringing their children or their grandchildren to watch a ballet that they remember with affection from their own childhood. The children are often dressed in their best party clothes, as befits a grand occasion, to watch the Stahlbaums' Christmas party, to hold their breath when the clock strikes and the mysterious Herr Drosselmeier enters with his nephew, to sit at the edge of their seats silently cheering the brave Nutcracker's fight with the Mouse King and admiring Marie's courage as she throws her slipper and wins the war for the good guys.

Each year, as thousands of girls watch the dancing snowflakes and flowers and admire the beautiful Sugar Plum Fairy, they dream about becoming ballerinas themselves. As thousands of boys watch the toy soldiers jump as high as any basketball player, or see the Cavalier snatch the Sugar Plum Fairy out of thin air to hold her securely on his shoulder, they learn that dancing is a demanding sport as well as an art form.

Each audience of children cheers the Nutcracker when he defeats the Mouse King and holds the King's crown high as a victory symbol. They cheer again when the Nutcracker, now turned into a handsome young prince, finishes telling his story in pantomime to the Sugar Plum Fairy. And at the end of the performance, when Marie and the Prince enter the sleigh with its reindeer and rise high above the stage to leave the Land of the Sweets, some of the younger children may shout as well as wave goodbye. Almost all of these children seem to know that *The Nutcracker* is different from a movie or a television show, that it deserves their full attention and respect because its creator, George Balanchine, had faith in them, their taste, and their good manners and gave them a true masterpiece that never condescends to a young audience.

Ballet historians have told us that the first *Nutcracker* ballet, with a score commissioned from Tchaikovsky and choreography created by Ivanov, was not a success when it was presented in St. Petersburg (now Leningrad) in 1892. Some of the critics in those days complained that the music was too much like a symphony and not enough like a dance score, and that there were far too many children in the cast to please an adult audience. Several also remarked with displeasure that there was not enough "real" dancing, that the ballerina did not even appear until the second act. But, apparently, even then the ballet was popular enough with audiences to remain in the reperatory continuously for thirty-seven years. Balanchine saw his first *Nutcracker* at the Maryinsky Theater in St. Petersburg and danced in it as a young student in the Imperial Ballet School. At first he was cast in minor roles, but eventually he danced the Nutcracker Prince. He remembered the prince's pantomime exactly and taught it himself to the innumerable young boys who would take the role in his version of the ballet many years later.

Nutcrackers are still danced in Russia today, but no longer in the Ivanov version. Various Russian choreographers have created ballets that are intended to show off the abilities of their top ballerinas and male dancers. So the child hero and heroine are performed by the adult stars of the company. And, for some strange reason, even the name of the heroine is changed: Marie has become Clara, which was actually, in the Hoffmann story, the name of her favorite doll.

There is, of course, nothing artistically inconsistent in taking the story even further away from its literary roots than Ivanov did. But all these new choreographers still insist on picturing Marie, her brother, and their young guests as "children," when they are actually danced by highly accomplished adults. Adults pretending to be children usually don't look childlike, but childish and coy. In one version, a young man who is about thirty years old rides a hobby horse around the room as the mischievous young Fritz. The scene is always unintentionally funny.

In Europe, versions of *The Nutcracker* that are closer to the Ivanov model have been presented now and then. Often, although Marie was danced by a child, the Nutcracker Prince was danced by an adult. That didn't work too well either. And somehow, in England, France, and Italy, those *Nutcrackers* never seemed to have much audience appeal and were usually dropped from the repertory after a few seasons.

More recently Rudolf Nureyev and Mikhail Barishnikov have created their own *Nutcracker* productions. Each originally danced the Nutcracker Prince himself, with a top ballerina as Marie. The Barishnikov version was danced for several seasons by the American Ballet Theater and was taped for television, where it was seen on one or more channels as a Christmas special for several years. It will probably be with us for some time, since the dancing in the TV version (with Barishnikov and a wonderful young ballerina, Gelsey Kirkland) is truly spectacular. However, the story is only distantly related to the original one: it concerns a young woman and man who fall in love and are separated by fate.

The Balanchine *Nutcracker,* which is the most lasting hit in dance history, was presented for the first time on February 2, 1954, by the New York City Ballet. Some critics reacted much like the ones in Ivanov's day. For instance, *The New York Times* reviewer John Martin complained about all those children on stage and regretted that he was forced to wait until the second act for any "real" dancing to begin. However, other critics loved it even then, and some realized that the very special dances Balanchine had made for the children were extraordinary and new: a way to use their best abilities and training without making them look like miniature adults, or presenting them as cute little tykes whom only relatives could admire. The children were *dancers* who still had much to learn before they could be considered professionals, but their steps had to be accurate and musical, their carriage dignified, and their stage manners impeccable.

Whatever the critics had to say, the New York public loved the ballet immediately and, since 1954, has bought almost every available ticket season after season.

Balanchine was asked why he had choreographed a ballet so different from his usual style, especially one that was so expensive to produce. He told ballet writer and former New York City Ballet dancer Nancy Reynolds: "It's my business to make repertories. I always say it's like a restaurant...you have to cook, you have to please lots of people. One person wants soup, one wants oysters. My approach to theater—to ballet—is to entertain the public." Balanchine, incidentally, was a superb and enthusiastic cook, who occasionally prepared memorable Russian feasts for his friends.

He also told Miss Reynolds that he knew about *The Nutcracker* because he had danced in it as a child in Russia. Why was the Christmas party so very *German* then? After all, he had certainly changed the Hoffmann story in other ways, so why not make it more Russian? He explained that "Russian Christmas is a German invention. They had German cakes and cookies, and German postcards with snow and little deer...very pretty. Also, it's very religious. Christ is born, so grown-ups never gave each other any presents out of respect for religion. But children were told beautiful stories about it. Our tree was full of food: chocolate, oranges, apples. You just pick up from the tree and eat. It's a tree of plenty. It represents food, plenty, life. We used to sing German Christmas songs all night...like 'Tannenbaum'. There was no Russian translation."[1]

Balanchine, of course, knew that many ballet critics would regard his *Nutcracker* as popular entertainment created to provide a sure-fire money-maker for the company, rather than as serious art. Many looked at this ballet as they would the annual Christmas pageant at the Radio City Music Hall or the Ice Capades, certain

[1]Reynolds, Nancy: *Repertory In Review: 40 Years Of The New York City Ballet,* p. 157

to fill seats, but of somewhat dubious artistic value as a major contribution to dance.

But Balanchine never made a distinction between what was popular and what was "artistic." As far as he was concerned, there were two kinds of dance: good and bad. A few years before he died, he told *New York Times* critic Anna Kisselgoff that he ranked his *Nutcracker* highly among his many works, indeed more highly than *Apollo,* generally considered to be one of his most innovative and important ballets.

There are, of course, other companies besides the New York City Ballet that dance *The Nutcracker.* All over the United States, from Maine to Florida, from New York to California, companies have their annual *Nutcracker* productions. These performances often provide the small local companies with much of their annual operating expenses, just as *Nutcracker* season contributes heavily to the income of the New York City Ballet.

In 1983, *Ballet News* reported that more than one thousand companies in the United States were doing *Nutcrackers* that year. Most of these productions were based on the Ivanov–Balanchine model, although some company artistic directors added a few choreographic details of their own.

In 1984, a very different *Nutcracker,* unlike any that had been performed since Tchaikovsky delivered his score to the Imperial Ballet, was created. In Seattle, Washington, the Pacific Northwest Ballet commissioned its artistic director, Kent Stowell, to choreograph a version closer to the original Hoffmann story, including the tale of Princess Pirlipat and her recovery from acute ugliness. Artist and author Maurice Sendak, who admired Hoffmann and did not like either the Balanchine or the Ivanov ballet, designed the scenery and costumes. Reviewers considered this production an interesting new approach, yet another contribution to the ever growing *Nutcracker* ballet repertory.

But it is the Balanchine ballet, with its warm, loving, traditional Stahlbaum family, its dancing children, its Christmas tree that seems to grow magically to the sky, its falling snow (which is carefully swept up by the stage crew at the end of the first act for reuse in the next performance), its swirling flowers, its loving, trusting, enterprising Marie, its brave Nutcracker prince, and its gracious, gentle, beautiful, regal Sugar Plum Fairy that will, most probably, still be with us when our children take their children to the annual Christmas performance.

Will the ballet change? Yes, of course. Balanchine is no longer with us to refine and polish each dancer's work at dress rehearsals, to explain to each new Marie how one curtsied in nineteenth century Germany and to each new Nutcracker Prince how to hold a sword and show him the exact meaning of each gesture in his pantomime. Some changes have crept in already. During the most recent performances, the children in the party scene were less formal, more like average American kids than like German children of the nineteenth century. One male guest actually had the audacity to put his arm around the waist of a parlor maid while she was serving him refreshments, a breach of decorum that would never have been permitted in the Stahlbaum household. Other subtler changes were evident in the dancing.

Ballet, unlike a musical score or a book, cannot be preserved with complete accuracy even with today's video tape possibilities. And Balanchine is no longer standing at his accustomed place in back of the left wing of the stage just out of the audience's view, watching over his dancers and correcting any missteps after each performance. But, essentially, there will probably be few changes because that's what the dancers and the audience want.

After one of *The Nutcracker*'s most recent performances,

principal dancer Patricia McBride, who has danced the Sugar Plum Fairy more often than any of the other ballerinas in the company today, was standing on the stage, a little out of breath, rubbing her foot in its tight little ballet slipper. A young dancer who had recently joined the corps came up to her and asked her why she held her arms a certain way during one of her solo variations. "Because that's the way Mr. Balanchine *likes* it," she said firmly, and in the present tense.

Balanchine may no longer be standing in the wings, but a few of the dancers who have been in the company the longest still turn their heads toward the left side of the stage as if they somehow expected to see him there, and audience and dancers sense his presence in that theater more than ever during *The Nutcracker* season. All of them want *The Nutcracker* to be performed the way he *likes* it... from now to the year 2000 and beyond.

THE
BALANCHINE
BALLET

As Performed by the Dancers
of the New York City Ballet Company

THE NUTCRACKER

CLASSICAL BALLET IN TWO ACTS, FOUR SCENES AND PROLOGUE

Music by Peter Ilyich Tchaikovsky

Choreography by George Balanchine

Scenery and Lighting by Rouben Ter-Artunian

Costumes by Karinska

DANCED BY THE NEW YORK CITY BALLET

Sugar Plum Fairy:		*Suzanne Farrell*
Cavalier:		*Peter Martins*
Dewdrop:		*Heather Watts*
Dr. Stahlbaum:		*Cornel Crabtree*
Their Children:	Marie	*Jordana Allen*
	Fritz	*Jonathan Joseph Pessolano*
Grandparents:		*Karin von Aroldingen and Bart Cook*
Herr Drosselmeier:		*Shaun O'Brien*
His Nephew (The Nutcracker):		*Timothy Lynch*
Soldier:		*Jean-Pierre Frolich*
Mouse King:		*Paul Sackett*
Hot Chocolate:		*Mel A. Tomlinson and Lauren Hauser*
Coffee:		*Wilhelmina Frankfurt*
Tea:		*Gen Horiuchi*
Candy Cane:		*Victor Castelli*
Marzipan Shepherdess:		*Stacy Caddell*

*and Members of The New York City Ballet and
Students at The School Of American Ballet*

It is Christmas Eve, in the year your grandmother's grandmother was nine years old. In the German town of Nuremberg, the newly fallen snow glistens on all the roofs and gables. The North Star shines so brightly that it reminds many of the people walking to family Christmas parties of the star that some had seen over Bethlehem the night Jesus was born. Some of the children even think that they see a Christmas angel hovering over the town to guard it from harm.

At the home of Dr. Stahlbaum, the Stahlbaum children, Marie and Fritz, have been waiting impatiently for the doors of the parlor to open to reveal the Christmas tree surrounded by their presents. In Germany, adults decorate the Christmas tree on Christmas Eve, and children are allowed to see it only when the real festivities begin. There are large family parties at which parents, grandparents, uncles, aunts, and cousins gather, along with a few close family friends, to celebrate together.

Marie and Fritz have been waiting for so long that they have both fallen asleep.

Marie, hearing the adults in the next room moving about to get everything ready for the party, wakes up and looks through the keyhole to see how things are progressing. She shakes her brother awake. Soon both are trying to get a glimpse of the tree and the presents, sometimes pushing each other out of the way to get a better view.

Finally, the guests begin to arrive. After everyone has been greeted and welcomed to the party, (Germans in those days were very formal and polite, even to relatives) the door to the parlor is opened, and everyone has a chance to admire the magnificently decorated tree. Of course, in those days there was no electricity, so the tree had real candles on it. Most of the decorations were homemade, too; especially the gingerbread men, chocolate soldiers, marzipan shepherdesses, and candy canes.

Since there are so many children at the party, the adults make sure
that the youngsters are entertained with games and dances so that they
won't get bored and into mischief. In those days, in Germany, boys often
played marching games, and both boys and girls were taught simple
dances, similar to those that their parents danced at balls. One dance game
that everybody loves looks a lot like "London Bridge Is Falling Down,"
and is led by Mrs. Stahlbaum and Fritz.

The arrival of the grandparents (as usual, bringing a few more cousins) is always a special event of the annual Christmas party. The children have been taught that the older members of the family deserve politeness and respect, as well as hugs and kisses, so everyone makes sure that the grandparents are comfortably settled in armchairs and served the most delicious refreshments before they distribute their presents. In those days, the gifts were almost always for the children, although they didn't get nearly as many then as some children get today. Most adults gave each other small gifts such as candy and flowers. Christmas was considered a family holiday on which everyone got together for a good time, rather than as an occasion to collect a lot of presents. However, this evening the grandparents receive some special presents from their grandchildren... probably some that they made themselves.

Games and dances continue until the clock strikes eight. At that
moment some of the children feel a suspenseful chill, even the lights in the
room seem to dim a little. A new guest arrives: Herr Drosselmeier, a
somewhat mysterious elderly gentleman, who is a very old friend of the
Stahlbaum family and Marie's godfather. As always, he has brought large
boxes of special toys he has invented for the children. This time he has
also brought his nephew, a handsome, well-mannered, but rather shy boy,
who helps his uncle carry in the presents.

Herr Drosselmeier sometimes enjoys surprising and startling the children, although perhaps he may not realize that he is also frightening some of the younger ones. He holds his long black cloak in front of his face, which makes him look like a very large bat. Even Marie is a little frightened until she realizes that this is her beloved godfather, whom she greets enthusiastically.

It is Herr Drosselmeier's habit to fix all of his friends' clocks whenever he visits, because clockmaking is one of his special hobbies. When he notices that the big grandfather clock, with its carved wooden owl on top, is about a minute slow, he pulls out his watchmaking tool and fixes it. Marie is introduced to the nephew. Like most little German girls in those days, she doesn't know many boys outside of the family, so she, too, is a little shy with the new visitor.

The children have learned from past parties that Herr Drosselmeier is not like most of the other people they know. He can be somewhat fussy and irritable, especially if there is a lot of noise. He seems to be a little hard of hearing, but he knows some wonderful magic tricks. The toys he invents are like nothing else in Nuremberg, or for that matter, anywhere else in the world. They are dolls, often as large as the children, that can march, jump, bow, and dance when he winds them up. Of course, today, wind-up toys are nothing special, but when your grandmother's grandmother was nine years old, no one but Herr Drosselmeier could make such toys. Indeed, the Stahlbaums valued them so highly that after the party they always locked them up in a big cabinet with glass doors and let the children play with them only with adult supervision, so that they could not get broken.

This year Herr Drosselmeier has brought three of his special dolls. First he unpacks a boy and girl clown (called Pierrot and Columbine), who can perform like ballet dancers.

*Then he takes a toy
soldier out of the third box.
This soldier not only marches
and kneels, he can even jump
high in the air and turn
while he is jumping.*

*After the three dolls have performed their acts, they are put back in
their boxes, to be stored later in the special cabinet. Now Herr
Drosselmeier produces his less delicate presents, the kind the children can
actually take back to their own toy boxes. First he brings out a hobby
horse. Every child in the room wants it. They start to fight over it, which
makes Herr Drosselmeier very nervous. So he organizes the children into
two teams. Each team gets to hold on to one end of the hobby horse, and
they pull in opposite directions. Whichever team wins gets to keep the
horse. The boys win when the girls fall over backwards with their legs in
the air, showing their pantalets and petticoats. That was a very shocking
thing to have happen in those very proper times. So, perhaps to keep
everyone from getting too upset, Herr Drosselmeier produces his very
special gift for this year's Christmas celebration.*

The gift is a large wooden doll, which, at first glance, looks like a rather ugly, wizened old man. Like the toy soldiers Fritz collects, he wears a brightly painted uniform. He has a large nose, slightly bulging eyes, a jutting chin, and lots of fine white hair on his head and in his

beard. The adults at the party know that the hair is made of spun glass, just like Herr Drosselmeier's wig...because Herr Drosselmeier is actually quite bald, although he would much prefer if nobody knew this.

Herr Drosselmeier holds up the special doll to attract the attention of the children, who are still arguing over the hobby horse; and one little girl notices first that this toy is different. Although he is not nearly as pretty as the dolls most of the girls have received as presents already, he has a very special talent: when a lever at the back of his head is moved up and down, he can open his large mouth, showing sharp teeth. With these teeth he can crack nuts. The doll is actually a nutcracker.

Herr Drosselmeier shows off the Nutcracker's ability, and the other children quickly gather around him, leaving the hobby horse lying unwanted on the floor.

As the children sit down to watch, Herr Drosselmeier (who never forgets anything) takes from his large pockets the nuts he has brought especially so that he can demonstrate his latest invention. His nephew, who has not joined in the games with the other children, now steps forward to help his uncle feed the Nutcracker the hard nuts and to distribute the soft nutmeats to the children. Of course, all want this special toy more than any others they have seen so far. But the present is for Marie, partly because she is, after all, Herr Drosselmeier's godchild and partly because she is his very favorite in the family.

This makes her brother Fritz so angry that he tears the Nutcracker from her arms, spins it around his head, drops it on the floor, and stomps on it. The Nutcracker is broken. His jaws have been dislodged so that he no longer can move them to crack nuts.

Herr Drosselmeier scolds Fritz and gives him a slight spank on the behind. But this punishment is really not needed. Poor Fritz feels very much ashamed of what he has done and retires, much subdued, into a corner of the room.

Herr Drosselmeier goes to comfort Marie, who is weeping over her injured Nutcracker. Although the inventor cannot restore his invention to its original glory, he does manage to bandage the broken jaw with a large white handkerchief he also happens to carry in his pocket for emergencies.

The other girls, with their dolls, gather around Marie. But the nephew has the most helpful idea: he brings over the new doll's bed Marie has received as a Christmas gift so that the wounded Nutcracker can get some much needed rest. Marie, realizing that the new boy understands better than anyone how she feels about this special toy and wants to do all he can to make her feel happy again, gratefully shakes his hand. Now they are friends.

As the girls rock their dolls, the boys are feeling restless. All of
them, except Herr Drosselmeier's nephew, come jumping and whooping
into the peaceful scene, including even Fritz, who has quickly forgotten
his bad conscience and his good intentions.

The parents realize that the children are getting tired and are
therefore not on their best behavior. The time has come for the traditional
ending of the Stahlbaums' annual Christmas Eve party: the grandfather's
dance. As has been the custom for as long as anyone in the family can
remember, each man presents his partner with a red rose on a velvet
cushion. The women, including the mother and the grandmother, attach
the flowers to their wrists with a red ribbon.

Then the adults do a slow and stately dance, which even the grandparents can still perform gracefully. On the other side of the room, the children do a similar dance, complete with roses for the girls.

Herr Drosselmeier's nephew has brought a red rose for Marie. He attaches it to her wrist, and they dance together.

*As the dance ends, the party is over. Most of the children don't
want to go home. They have had such a wonderful time. One small
cousin even tries to hide under Marie's skirt, hoping that nobody will
notice her; but of course her parents find her and take her home.*

*Herr Drosselmeier also does not seem to want to leave. He is lost
in a dream world of his own, until his nephew gently reminds him that it
is time to go.*

*Marie and her new friend say goodbye. Both are sorry that their
time together is over so soon.*

Now the house is dark, and the children are supposed to be in bed.
But Marie cannot sleep. She just doesn't want the evening to end. So she
steals back into the parlor, finds the Nutcracker in his bed under the tree,
and settles down with him on the couch. There, her, mother who has been
looking for, her finds her asleep in her thin cotton nightgown. It has
started to snow, and the room is getting chilly, so she covers Marie with
a warm, knitted shawl.

As Marie sleeps, Herr Drosselmeier comes back into the dimly lit room, looking for the Nutcracker under the tree. He finds it in the girl's arms, gently removes it, and uses his watch-fixing tool to repair the broken jaw. He takes off the bandage and moves the lever. The Nutcracker is repaired. He gives it one more reassuring twist with the tool, which, in the strange light, looks almost like a magic wand. Then he replaces the Nutcracker next to Marie on the couch and leaves very quietly.

Suddenly there are strange noises all over the house. Marie wakes up with a start. She looks out of the window at the falling snow, rubs her bare arms to get warmer, and crawls back under the woolen shawl.

The owl on top of the large clock seems to be transformed into Herr Drosselmeier perched in the air, flapping his long black cloak so that he looks more than ever like a bat. He also makes all kinds of strange movements, something like the ones he makes when he is irritated or annoyed by too much commotion. Behind him his shadow on the wall looks huge, making him into a very frightening figure. Marie briefly hides behind the curtain.

When she comes out again, the house is noisier than ever, full of creaks and cracks and groans. Suddenly, out of nowhere, a huge mouse appears, looks around the room, turns, and leaves by the back door. Of course it could not get out through its usual hole, since it is over six feet tall. Within seconds more mice appear. Three of them crowd around Marie, who pushes them away.

Marie has, of course, always known that there were mice in the house. They are in almost every house in Nuremberg; that is the reason her parents keep a large, strong brown cat. But the mice she has seen before were more like three inches tall, not six feet. Unlike some little girls, she is not afraid of mice in a more usual size, but these huge creatures are enough to scare even a very brave person.

After the giant mice have, temporarily, disappeared again, everything becomes even more strange and frightening. The furniture in the room grows and grows. The cabinet for Fritz's toy soldiers is now as big as a house, and the soldiers themselves are taller than Marie, except

*for the drummer boy, who is a few inches shorter. He turns out to look a
lot like one of her stuffed rabbits.*

*And then the tree starts growing and growing, up into the sky.
Even the ornaments get bigger and bigger. The candy canes and the
marzipan figures are now as big as Marie. Really frightened, she runs to
lean over her Nutcracker in his bed, to protect him from harm.*

*But the bed moves magically away from her, out of sight, and in its
place a human-sized bed appears, with a large Nutcracker, who seems to
be about as tall as Herr Drosselmeier's nephew.*

*And now the mice come back...in hordes. The big mice have even
brought their children along, and every one of them is taller than Marie.*

*Although Marie has been brought up to believe that all well-
mannered girls are quiet and gentle and never fight, she really has a great
deal of courage and spirit. She is not at all like the helpless little creatures*

5 0

German girls were supposed to be when your grandmother's grandmother was nine years old. With all those huge mice seeming to take control of her home, she decides that she must fight to protect herself, her toys, and her sleeping family.

She wakes the Nutcracker, who somehow has managed to sleep through the whole commotion. Together they take command of the toy soldiers and order them to attack and drive out the mice.

The soldier's bullets don't seem to hurt the mice. Not even the cannon (which has grown to life size along with the rest of Fritz's toy army) can intimidate the enemy. It shoots its ammunition, but the mice seem to think the cannon balls are made of cheese. They just pick them up and nibble on them happily. And, in a counterattack, they pick up the toy soldiers, several soldiers to each mouse, and carry them away.

The Nutcracker now joins the fight in earnest, pulling his sword and going after the mouse invaders. But a brand-new and even more threatening character appears on the scene. He is definitely the mouse-in-charge. He is twice as big as the rest of the mice and has seven heads, each topped with a glittering crown. The Nutcracker attacks the Mouse King, but the huge creature is soon getting the best of the fight. Although the super mouse has a large, flabby stomach, and his extra heavy body and seven heads seem to make him look unbalanced and unsteady on his rather small feet, he is still so much bigger than the Nutcracker that almost at once he has his small opponent on the ground, fighting for his life.

The Nutcracker tries every move he can think of. At one point he even attaches himself to the Mouse King's back, hoping to topple him, but the huge enemy just shakes him off.

With the Nutcracker again on the ground, fighting off the Mouse King, who threatens any second to overwhelm, him, Marie decides that the time has come for her to take a more active part in the battle. She has no weapon except her slipper. She takes it off and hurls it at the Mouse King with all her strength, hitting him squarely in the back. Of course, the slipper really can't hurt him, but it distracts him from his fight with the Nutcracker.

He turns to Marie to punish her for her daring, and she runs to the
bed in the corner, with the Mouse King running after her, waving his
large sword. He stands over her, brandishing his weapons, but he has
made a serious mistake. He has forgotten all about the Nutcracker, who
rushes after him and plunges his own sword into the fierce creature's
heart, wounding him mortally.

The Mouse King staggers backwards and falls dead on the floor. Now the Nutcracker cuts off the Mouse King's most glittering crown, and walks slowly to the bed where Marie is lying. Meanwhile, the other mice are carrying their fallen king away. They have lost the war.

The Nutcracker walks slowly toward the large windows, holding
the crown high above his head, and the windows open to show a
glistening, shining snow-filled world outside.

As the walls of the house disappear to be replaced by snow-laden
pines the Nutcracker walks on, proudly holding up the crown.

Marie, exhausted from the battle, has gone to sleep and does not notice that the bed, pulled by an unseen force, is following the Nutcracker out into the snow. She goes on sleeping, even though, in her thin cotton nightgown and with only one slipper, she should be feeling very cold. But the weather does not seem to disturb her, even though the snowflakes are falling faster and thicker in a whirling wind.

As the snow becomes heavier, and the wind quiets down, the flakes look like white bits of cotton, and the scene is very peaceful, with Marie lying in her bed and the North Star shining brightly.

But another miracle is about to happen. The Nutcracker enters. He stands for a moment, as if enchanted, holding up the crown. Suddenly, without warning, he is transformed into a beautiful young prince, who looks a great deal like Herr Drosselmeier's nephew. But, of course, he is wearing much more beautiful clothes than an ordinary German boy would wear to a family Christmas party. He has on a velvet suit, embroidered with silver, just the kind of garment that a prince would wear for a very special occasion.

He approaches the bed in which Marie is still sleeping. She
wakes up, and he kneels down and kisses her hand. After all, she has
saved his life. Then, as a reward, he places the crown he has won in the
battle on her head. It glistens in the moonlight.

As one looks closer, each snowflake seems to turn into a beautiful young princess, twirling and dancing in the breeze.

Hand-in-hand Marie and the Prince walk into the winter wonderland, with the evening star lighting their way. Marie and her Nutcracker Prince are going to the Land of the Sweets, a country where the sun always shines, the streets are paved with candy, and the palaces and towers are made of cake, gingerbread, and other good things to eat. It's also a place where there are never any angry words exchanged, and where everyone is treated with kindness, good humor, and respect. The inhabitants come from all corners of the real world and the world of the imagination; they communicate with each other through dance. Dancing is a language without words that everybody can understand.

*The Land of the Sweets
is ruled by the Sugar Plum Fairy,
a beautiful, kind, and gracious
princess. Before meeting her
two guests, she is dancing with
a whole choir of Christmas
angels.*

*Marie and the Prince arrive
in a small sailboat, which was
sent to fetch them. They
are met by the Sugar Plum Fairy
and her subjects.*

64

After greeting his hostess, the Prince describes the past night's adventures.

So that everyone will be able to understand his story, he uses dance steps and gestures to tell his story.

You

and you listen.

I will tell you everything.

Just wait.

I slept, and she comforted me.

All of a sudden I saw

with my two eyes

a mouse, and then another mouse.

What shall I do?

I called my soldiers to fight.

Then came the King of the Mice.

He asked me to fight, and I accepted.

He pushed me back.

Marie threw her shoe.

The King of the Mice turned, and I killed him.

Victory.

Now I have told you everything.

The Sugar Plum Fairy is pleased and astonished at the courage of
the two guests who apparently were willing to endanger their own lives
for each other. "You have won my heart," she tells them in an
unmistakable gesture.

They are led to a special throne, a place of honor, where they are
served delicious food and are invited to watch the many dances to be
performed by the citizens of the Land of the Sweets.

The first group of dancers is dressed in Spanish costumes. They represent hot chocolate, which Marie and the Prince are now drinking. After their exhausting fight and the walk through the snowy woods, that hot drink certainly tastes good.

For any adults who might be visiting the magical country, there is coffee, represented by a dancer in an Arabian costume.

And tea, impersonated by two Chinese girls in pigtails and a boy
with a straw hat who can jump higher than anyone Marie and the Prince
have ever seen.

Next come
the Sugar Canes in
their striped suits. They
are led by a very
athletic young man
who can jump through
a whirling hoop.

Then comes a group of marzipan shepherdesses, who look like some of the decorations on the Stahlbaums' tree. So they might actually be from Nuremberg too!

The next person to enter is a very large woman with a fan, a mirror, and a huge hoop skirt. She reminds Marie of the Woman Who Lived in a Shoe; but, of course, she is much too big to live in such a small apartment. However, she does seem to have many children, who come running out from under her skirt. They are dressed like boy and girl clowns, rather like the two wind-up dolls Herr Drosselmeier had brought to the Christmas party. Under the approving eyes of the woman (who is called "Mother Ginger"), they do their own special dance; then they run back under that huge skirt, as Mother Ginger leaves to the enthusiastic applause of the two guests of honor.

The most beautiful group of dancers comes last: young women who are dressed like roses and violets in pink and light purple gowns. Among these flowers, gleaming like a diamond, a dewdrop floats, soars, and twirls.

While the special performance for the two guests is underway, the Sugar Plum Fairy has quietly retired to her castle to change into her special dancing dress, the most beautiful costume in her wardrobe. She returns with a handsome young man from her court (known as the Cavalier) to perform for the children.

Each has a special dance.

And then they dance together.

Unfortunately, even the most wonderful party must come to an end. But special transportation has again been arranged for the guests of honor. A sleigh, pulled by reindeer, arrives. The Sugar Plum Fairy bids the children goodbye, and while the citizens of the Land of the Sweets wave and cheer, Marie and the Prince ride high into the sky, away from the magical country.

Where are they going? They don't really know, but they are sure that the Sugar Plum Fairy has arranged everything well.

So, of course, Marie is not surprised when, after a trip high above the clouds where nobody could see the sleigh, she somehow lands right back in her own bed, in her room in Nuremberg, on Christmas morning.

Later she will tell her parents, her brother, and all of her best friends about her great adventure. All will assure her that she has had a wonderful dream...that actually she was at home in her bed all the time.

But she will never believe them. She is sure that the fight with the Mouse King, the transformation of the Nutcracker into the Prince, her trip through the snowy woods to the Land of the Sweets, with all its dancing citizens and its ruler, the Sugar Plum Fairy, really happened. She also knows that she and the Nutcracker prince (who looks so much like Herr Drosselmeier's nephew) will be good friends forever.

What do you think?

THE NUTCRACKER CHARACTERS

As the Dancers See Them

The characters in any ballet, even a story ballet like The Nutcracker, have to express themselves through dance steps and certain programmed gestures (called mime). Since they don't talk (like the actors in a play, a movie, or on television), they have to *show* you what kinds of people they are supposed to be rather than *tell* you. Of course, that is a very special skill.

Usually all the principal characters in the New York City Ballet's *Nutcracker* can act as well as dance, so that the audience gets a very good impression of what Marie, Fritz, Herr Drosselmeier, his nephew, and even the grandparents, who have short but important parts, are supposed to be like.

But this seemed like a very good opportunity to allow the dancers who play those parts to *talk* about their characters, when usually they can only dance and mime them. So, here, in order of appearance are the *real* people describing the *stage* people whom they become in the ballet.

Jordana Allen (*Marie*)

I think Marie is a little younger than I am...perhaps nine years old. I am actually eleven. In many ways she is a lot like me. She wants to be graceful and polite, but she can lose her temper at times; for instance, when her brother teases her too much. She is probably a lot stronger and more athletic than she looks... also like me. Before I started taking ballet classes seriously, I played a lot of softball on a Little League team. That is one of the reasons I hardly ever miss when I throw my slipper at the Mouse King. I hurl it like a baseball. Some other Maries always seem to miss the Mouse King, even though he is a very large target. One Marie even threw the slipper into the orchestra. Once it went right into a musician's tuba. I think he had to blow it out.

But although, in the beginning, Marie is just a regular girl, she later proves that she has more courage, imagination, and determination than most girls her age.

She is, of course, scared of all those large mice. Who wouldn't be? But she doesn't run away or hide under the bed. She helps the Nutcracker defeat the Mouse King and protects her home. She doesn't stand around and wait for him to rescue her, like most princesses in fairy tales usually do. She cooperates to help him win the fight. That's the reason, I think, that the Sugar Plum Fairy is so impressed with *both* of them.

Adults who don't understand the ballet are always telling me that I am supposed to be in love with the Nutcracker Prince, and he with me. I think that's dumb. We are both much too young to be in love. But I think that by the time we have been through all those adventures together, we will be friends forever. And very good friends are important in one's life.

Also, people suggest that Marie just dreamed the story about the Mouse King and the Land of the Sweets when she went to bed after the Christmas party. I'm not sure, because, in a way the Christmas party is like a dream, too. Most of us have never been to a party like that, where a whole large family gets together—parents, grandparents, uncles, aunts, cousins...all those relatives— and where everybody seems to love everybody else so much. That's why that party sometimes makes me a little sad.

Anyway, most of the time I don't believe that the Mouse King and the Sugar Plum Fairy's adventures were just a dream, although most adults think so. Someone told me backstage that Mr.

Balanchine didn't think it was a dream either, that the adventures actually happened to Marie. And, since he invented the whole story, he must be right.

Jonathan Joseph Pessolano (*Fritz*)

Everybody always describes Fritz as a brat. I don't think he is a brat. I think he is looking for attention a

89

lot of the time. And to me that seems only natural. After all, Marie gets a lot more attention than he does. Also, she gets all the good presents: not only the Nutcracker, but a doll, and even the hobby horse, which to me seems more like a present that's meant for a boy. All along she gets her way, and Fritz is ignored unless he does something he shouldn't, like pulling one of the girls' hair ribbons.

Personally, I think that children often behave the way adults expect them to behave. Everybody seems to think that Fritz is a brat, so he behaves like one some of the time.

But, underneath it all, I think he really wants to be a good person. When he breaks the Nutcracker because he is furious that Herr Drosselmeier, like everybody else, seems to prefer Marie to him, he is terribly sorry.

I think he's probably a perfectly normal, nice boy, who is just a little immature. When he grows up, he'll probably turn out very well. He may even become an important man like his father.

Karin von Aroldingen
(Grandmother)

The Stahlbaum grandmother is very kind and sweet. She is also old-fashioned in the nicest possible way. Today's grandmothers may be busy with careers of their own: they might run a business or be teachers or doctors or lawyers. But in Marie's day, German grandmothering was probably a full-time job. Grandmothers knitted and sewed for their grandchildren. They read them bedtime stories, and they were always there when they were needed. They were important in carrying on many family traditions from one generation to the next.

I think that this particular grandmother is important to everyone in the family. She is accorded a great deal of respect as well as love; Mr. Balanchine showed us this in the family scenes he created for the ballet. Also, when children don't behave exactly as they should, a grandmother can just smile and talk to one of the other grandchildren. The parents, of course, have to discipline the boy or girl who behaves badly. So the grandparents don't have to get involved when Fritz starts having fights over toys and pulls the girls' hair. They can count on Dr. and Mrs. Stahlbaum to handle the situation. They brought up their own children to be considerate of other people and to have good manners, so now they can count on them

to do the same for Marie and Fritz. Like most grandparents, they can have a lot of fun with their grandchildren and leave the discipline mainly to the mother and father.

Bart Cook (*Grandfather*)

Although the grandfather does not get to do a lot on stage as a dancer, or even an actor, the character is very important to the meaning and the mood of the story. In Balanchine's staging of the first act, he makes it quite clear that the Stahlbaums are a close, loving, and very

91

traditional family, in which everyone holds his or her own special place.

This becomes obvious when the grandparents enter and instantly seem to be the center of attention. We get the feeling that the family has behaved in this manner for generations past and will continue to behave so in generations to come.

The last dance, which ends the party, is called "The Grandfather Dance." I think we are supposed to realize that the grandfather was taught that dance by his own grandfather, and that he had taught it to his son, who will teach it to his children. It's a family tradition that is expected to continue through the generations.

All of that fits in very well with ballet concepts, which are also built on tradition, with one generation of dancers teaching their roles to the next.

Shaun O'Brien
(Herr Drosselmeier)

I think of Herr Drosselmeier more in terms of character and personality than in terms of background and occupation. After all the years I have performed him, I have not yet figured out what he did before he came to the party, or what he does when he leaves. Perhaps we are not even supposed to know what his past and future are.

In a way he is like the Drosselmeier in the original E.T.A. Hoffmann story, though none of the other characters in the ballet are. He is mysterious and strange, but is also very rational, actually sometimes very wise. He may seem quirky and eccentric, and some of his movements may seem unlike those made by the other people in the ballet, but he is also kind and generous. Later, when I am sitting on the clock, when Marie wakes up on the couch, I accentuate those strange movements, so that I remind her of the owl on the clock and of a bat. That frightens her...but I am never a character out of a horror story. I know (even if she does not) that everything will turn out well for her in the end.

I also think that many of the adults at the party consider Drosselmeier stranger and weirder than many of the children do. Children like him, especially Marie. With adults, he is either withdrawn or polite in an exaggerated way. With children he is much more natural. He wants to impress them. That may be one of the reasons he wears those gold chains and bangles. He knows that children find that kind of glittering jewelry fascinating.

But even though he likes the children, he is uncomfortable in the middle of a crowd. When the children get too close, he gets nervous and upset. The children seem to know this instinctively...they seem, deliberately, to leave some space around him.

Also, I feel that the party reminds him of something in his own, mysterious past. When couples are dancing, he doesn't join in. He stands in the background and moves his arms and hands as if he were directing the dance. When the little girls rock their dolls, he looks rather sad, as if he were remembering someone he has lost...his mother, perhaps. And, at the end of the party, he seems absorbed in the same kind of feelings. He may be remembering a party from his youth, when he was not so alone and isolated.

He obviously cares about his nephew and treats him more like an adult than like one of the other children. But I think that the nephew doesn't live with him; that, perhaps, he only visits him over the Christmas holidays.

He is not a father figure to him, more like an equal. There are many similarities in the personalities of the nephew and the uncle: the shyness, the withdrawal from noisy crowds, the dislike of childish quarrels. And Drosselmeier wants his nephew to like Marie and to get to know her, because he likes her.

In shaping the stage character, I have also patterned some of my movements on those of Mr. Balanchine. There was a space around him, too. He was very polite, even formal at times. So, some of my memories of Mr. Balanchine may show up in the way I play Drosselmeier.

Incidentally, Mr. Balanchine allowed me to shape the character the way I saw him, most of the time. But sometimes I would do something he did not like, that did not fit his own perception of Drosselmeier. For instance, in one performance I burped loudly when I swallowed one of the nuts, and Mr. Balanchine let me know that he didn't want me to do that. I think he didn't want Drosselmeier to look ridiculous. He was supposed to be dignified even when he was quirky. That accentuated his mystery.

Timothy Lynch (*Herr Drosselmeier's Nephew / the Nutcracker Prince*)

Herr Drosselmeier's nephew is a rather mysterious boy. He doesn't even seem to have a name...at least nobody calls him hy a name. He is different from all the other children in the room, although he seems to be only a little

94

older than most of them. His behavior is more mature, and he spends most of his time either by himself or with the adults at the party.

I think he is very shy and not used to being around children his own age. He's probably an only child...perhaps even an orphan. And he is very sensitive. He likes taking care of other people. For instance, he is the one person at the party who knows how upset Marie really is about the broken Nutcracker, so he brings over the bed.

Also, he is very helpful to his uncle. He assists him in demonstrating the mechanical toys and putting them back into the boxes; and he also helps his uncle demonstrate the Nutcracker. He doesn't join in any of the fights and arguments with the other children or try to get any of the toys for himself. He doesn't seem to want any. Of all the boys, he is the only one who doesn't even get a paper hat.

When the party breaks up, he makes sure that his uncle knows it is time to leave, since Herr Drosselmeier often seems lost in his own world and needs someone to pull him back into reality.

But just because the boy is gentle, kind, and polite does not mean he is weak or afraid to be himself. He shows that he is rather strong when he helps to carry those heavy boxes with the mechanical toys. And he shows that he is good at some kinds of sports because he certainly dances better than any of the other boys at the party.

So when he becomes the courageous Nutcracker, who can even take on the huge Mouse King with his sword, he doesn't really change. He still wants to take care of people, like the toy soldiers and Marie, only now he has to do it in a different way...by using his body, not just his mind. He doesn't change when he becomes the Prince either. Other qualities in his character show up more: his grace and his very good manners. When he demonstrates to the Sugar Plum Fairy how he defeated the Mouse King, he shows that he has a sense of humor.

I agree with Jordana that

the Prince does not fall in love with Marie. They are both too young for that, but adults sometimes think it's cute for children to look as if they are in love. I don't think any of the children on *The Nutcracker* are supposed to be cute. Mr. Balanchine meant all of us to have grace and dignity...like all of the other dancers on the stage.

Jean-Pierre Frohlich
(Toy Soldier)

I am one of the few dancers in the company who started out as Fritz, became the Nutcracker Prince, and stayed with the New York City Ballet to become a professional dancer. During one *Nutcracker* season I usually dance several parts: Tea, the Toy Soldier, and Candy Cane. Every one of these characters requires a different ballet style. As the Tea, I do what's known as character dancing: standard ballet steps and movement, often with some special national or folk dance overtones. In Tea I dance a Chinese character.

The Toy Soldier requires a different approach. I am not a person, but a doll, and that means I have to keep my body stiff and straight. Dolls don't have a lot of joints. Sometimes I almost feel that I have to stop breathing to look properly doll-like. Mr. Balanchine used dancing dolls in several ballets. The best known is *Coppelia*.

Candy Cane is very athletic. We really have to jump high and move fast as we pass through that hoop. And we also have to remember that we are dancers and keep our toes pointed.

When I danced the Nutcracker Prince, Mr. Balanchine still coached us himself. We learned the steps from one of our teachers, but he put the final polish on our performance. Incidentally, I was the first Prince to wear black patent leather shoes, rather than white soft dancing slippers. While I was doing my pantomime, Mr. Balanchine looked at one of the girls from the corps who was watching rehearsals that day. She was wearing shiny black shoes. He asked her to take them off and lend them to me. Then he asked me to continue dancing wearing them. They were much too big; I had to stuff them with Kleenex so they would not fall off my feet. But Mr. Balanchine said they looked much better, more like the dancing shoes that men wore at the royal court in France during the time of Louis XIV. "Not so much like bedroom slippers", he said. So the next day I went to be fitted for patent leather dancing pumps. And Nutcracker princes have been wearing that kind of shoes ever since.

Suzanne Farrell
(*The Sugar Plum Fairy*)

The Sugar Plum Fairy is the ruler of the Kingdom of the Sweets. She is the main character there, not the Prince with whom she dances at the end.

Mr. Balanchine carries this concept over from the first act where Marie is the real heroine, the reason for the whole ballet. The Sugar Plum Fairy is, in a way, an adult extension of Marie.

The first act, of course, is a party in the *real* world. The children act like children having a good time. But when Marie is given the Nutcracker,

something changes. She seems to realize that this doll could make a difference in her whole life, which, of course, it does.

After the party ends, everything is still real, but it becomes bigger than life. Marie, although she does not grow physically, grows up in knowledge and understanding. She chooses to accept the help of the Nutcracker, and she puts her trust in him blindly. We all must do that at times, when we care deeply about someone. And he trusts her and accepts her help.

Actually I see trust as the most important part of their relationship. There is no time for either to ask, "Do I really trust this person? Do I want to get involved?" They are committed to caring for each other and helping each other from the beginning. That is why they are invited to go to the Sugar Plum Fairy's kingdom and to have all those wonderful experiences.

The Sugar Plum Fairy is obviously in charge in the Land of the Sweets. She has all the authority. She is an elegant lady, beautiful and kind; and

even though she is the ruler, she does not make anyone feel inferior or unworthy. There are children and adults in her kingdom, and she treats all of them with dignity. Manners and poise are required by all — always.

Mr. Balanchine treated all human beings with respect, including children. He never talked down to them, or for that matter choreographed down to them. He dealt with all people at their highest level and assumed that they would behave at that level. And that is what the Sugar Plum Fairy does too.

I think there is a real moral to this ballet, as there is in many fairy tales. Because Marie is trusting and loving, she is able to grow toward new horizons. She is offered an adventure, a chance to show her best qualities, and she accepts the opportunity. She does not shy away. She does not know that she will be rewarded if she does what is right. Although the visit to the Land of the Sweets seems to be the reward, the acceptance of Marie's commitment in Act I (which meant that she was fulfilling her highest potential) was actually the true reward. She does what she does because she is a special person. And, in the Sugar Plum Fairy, she sees the kind of person she might be when she grows up, with the same qualities of friendship, graciousness, generosity, and nobility.

It is interesting that the children who played Marie and the Nutcracker Prince said that what their characters felt for each other was friendship and trust. It is not easy to be a good friend. You have to make sacrifices. That is a very good lesson for life.

Marie will carry the lessons she learned back into her everyday existence. We hope that she may be able to pass them on the others. After you have had a really extraordinary experience, you can never be the same again. You have to let it influence you...and like Marie, you will become a better, more loving person.

Peter Martins
(*The Cavalier*)

A cavalier in a ballet is a grand and handsome young man who looks like a prince and gets to dance with the ballerina. He is the kind of partner a young girl would want to take her to her first important dance.

Cavaliers often don't have a specific part to act. They must, however, be very fine dancers so that they can perform difficult and complicated solos (called "variations" in ballet

99

language). Most of all, they must be the kind of partners who make the ballerina look wonderful...even better than she does when she dances by herself.

Heather Watts (*Dewdrop*)

The Dewdrop is different from the flowers. For one, the flowers don't leave the stage. They are constantly swirling around, forming different kinds of groupings. But the Dewdrop is really like a drop of water...like dew on flowers. It's there, and then suddenly it's gone. You see it glistening and catching the light, and then you suddenly don't see it.

I think the last pose is very significant. The Dewdrop is there in the center with the flower dancers all around it. The picture has changed from a whole garden of flowers, with the Dewdrop falling from one blossom to the next, to the image of one perfect flower, with the Dewdrop gleaming like a diamond at the center.

Technically, it's not one of the most difficult pieces I've danced, but it takes a lot of stamina and strength. You have five entrances. After the first two, when you have turned and jumped, you are already a little tired. You have to rush backstage from one side to the other to get back on. Then you have your big entrance, where you dance diagonally from the back to the front of the stage. By that time I am sometimes a little out of breath. Then you have to run around in back again, and come out to do all those really big, spectacular jumps.

As a choreography, the Waltz of the Flowers is one of my favorites. I really love it, and I think the audience does, too.

BIBLIOGRAPHY

Balanchine, George and Mason, Francis: *Complete Stories of the Great Ballets,* Doubleday, Garden City, New York, 1978

Chappell, Warren: *The Nutcracker* (Based on the Alexander Dumas, père, version) Alfred Knopf, New York, 1958

Crocce, Arlene: *Afterimages,* Vintage Books, New York, 1977

Crowle, Pigeon and Davis, Mike: *The Nutcracker Ballet,* Faber and Faber, Ltd., London, 1958

Denby, Edwin: *Dancers, Buildings and People in the Streets,* Popular Library, New York, 1965

Gruen, John: *The World's Great Ballets*, H. Abrams, Inc., New York, 1976

Hoffmann, E.T.A.: *Nutcracker,* Crown Publishers, New York, 1984 (Translation by Ralph Manheim from the German *The Nutcracker and the Mouse King*)

Kirstein, Lincoln: *Lincoln Kirstein's Thirty Years, The New York City Ballet,* Alfred Knopf, New York, 1978

Reynolds, Nancy: *Repertory in Review*, Dial Press, New York, 1977

Additional material from the New York City Ballet, the New York Museum of Broadcasting, and the New York City Library for the Performing Arts Dance Collection at Lincoln Center.

Photography Credits